The Little Angel Books Series

Happy Feet

A Child's Guide
to Foot Reflexology

Written & Illustrated
by Leia A. Stinnett

Cover art by Leia Stinnett

ISBN 0-929385-88-8

Published by

StarChild Press
a division of

Light Technology
Publishing
P.O. Box 1526
Sedona, Arizona 86339
(520) 282-6523

Printed by

**MISSION
POSSIBLE
Commercial
Printing**

P.O. Box 1495
Sedona, AZ 86339

Happy Feet

A Child's Guide
to Foot Reflexology

our feet are a very important part of your body. They help you stand up. They help you walk. They help you run and jump. They support the weight of your entire body.

Sometimes after a lot of walking or exercise, your feet feel tired. They may hurt or ache. You might find yourself rubbing them, or asking your mom or dad or a friend to rub them for you.

Did you know that when you rub your feet, you are also helping your eyes, ears, sinuses, heart, lungs, stomach, kidneys, intestines — all of your internal organs, your bones, muscles and nerves?

Did you know that by rubbing your feet, you are helping all these important parts of your body stay healthy?

On the bottom and top of your feet are about 72,000 little points called **reflex points**.

When you rub or push on these points, energy is sent to a particular nerve, gland, organ or muscle in your body, carrying with it a special message:

Unwanted feelings are now moving out of my body; good feelings are now moving into my body. My body is strong, healthy and in balance.

This type of healing work is called **reflexology**. Reflexology is a very old method of helping people feel better. The ancient Egyptians used foot reflexology in treating problems in the body as early as the year 2330 B.C.

The type of reflexology used today was founded in the 1930s by a woman therapist named Eunice Ingham.

She discovered that sore or

tender spots on the bottom of her clients' feet somehow related to places in their bodies that were not feeling well.

By pressing on the sore places on the bottoms of peoples' feet, Eunice found her clients getting healthier and healthier.

OW!
MY
EYE
IS
SORE!

Today Reflexology is used by different types of health practitioners, mainly people who are interested in helping people get well without having to use drugs and medications.

By working on the feet once

a week, or perhaps several times depending on what the person's complaint is, the person's body comes back into balance and the health problem is eliminated.

How to Do Foot Reflexology

There are many different ways to use your fingers, knuckles and thumbs to work on the bottom of your feet.

First, you can simply rub your feet. Just rubbing the different areas of your feet will help your body become more balanced.

An easy method for you to learn is called **thumb walking**.

Thumb walking works very well, but it does take a bit of practice.

Your thumb is very strong, so it is often the first choice as a tool in the reflexology treatment.

Keep your thumb bent as in the picture. Lift it up and down, up and down, pressing in on the bottom of your foot, then lifting your thumb up and bringing the thumb back down in a new place on the bottom of your foot.

You want to take tiny little "steps" with your thumb, so you

can cover as much of the bottom of your foot as possible
while your thumb "goes for a
walk."

Comparing the Foot Reflexes to Your Body

Imagine that you are standing
up. Your feet are standing up
next to you with the heel
touching the floor. One foot is
on each side of your body.
Your toes are pointed up
toward the top of your head.

As in the picture to the right,
you can see that *your toes are
like your head.* The place where
your toes join your feet are like
your neck.

The upper part of your feet
reflect your chest and upper

back, including all the organs
and bones and muscles you
find in this part of your body.

The arch of your feet from
one side to the other would be
the same as your stomach and
middle back, and all the
organs, bones, muscles and
nerves in that area.

The heels of your feet represent your hip area and your lower back.

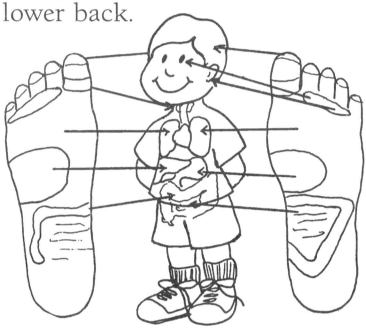

Look at the picture above. Can you see how the different parts of your body are located on the bottom of your feet in about the same place that you find them in your body?

Let's travel through your body and take a look at each

organ and gland, one at a time. You will learn how it works in the body and see where the reflex point for that organ is located on your feet.

Now press down on the area of the outside edge of your foot. Begin at the little toe and press all the way down to your heel. This is the area that corresponds with the **lymph system**. Thus, by pressing on this part of your foot, you are helping your body get rid of waste materials.

Work all around the areas of both ankles and across the top of your foot where your leg joins your foot. This area helps your **lower back**, your **hips**, your **knees** and your **reproductive organs**.

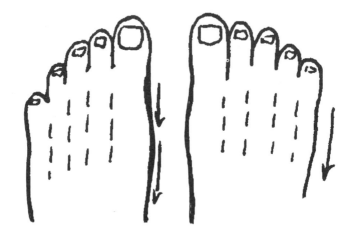

Work the places between each toe on top of your foot, from the place where your toes connect with your foot, to where your ankles join your legs.

The places that you work on the top of your feet cover the

same reflexes for the body that you worked on the bottom of your feet. In this way, you are giving your body a little extra special attention.

How do your feet feel?
Are they happy now?

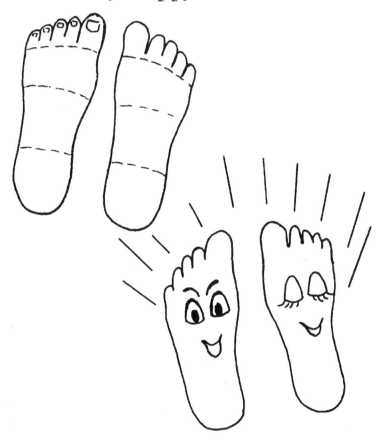

The area between the solar plexus and the beginning of your heel area contains many important organs —

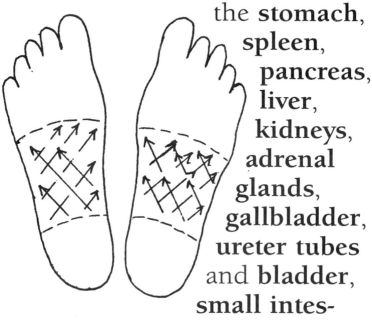

the **stomach**, **spleen**, **pancreas**, **liver**, **kidneys**, **adrenal glands**, **gallbladder**, **ureter tubes** and **bladder**, **small intestine** and part of the **large intestine**. This area needs to be covered well in working on your feet.

Start at the beginning of the arch area and move down to the edge of your heel area. Work in strips from top to bottom until you feel you have pressed on the entire area.

Now, work from the top of your heel area to the edge of your heel. Work across the heel also. This is usually a very tough area to work. However, it has important organs such as the **small** and **large intestines**, which help to eliminate waste products from the body.

Work the whole heel area.

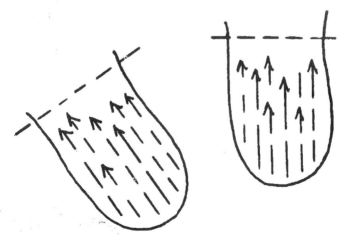

Now, work down the inside edge of your foot, from the top of your big toe to the tip of your heel. This is your **spine**. Give it a lot of love.

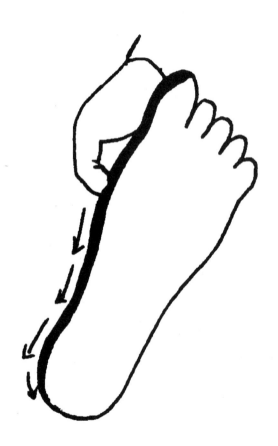

As you can see in the picture below, the **thyroid** and **parathyroid glands** are located at the place where your big toes connect to the top portion of your foot.

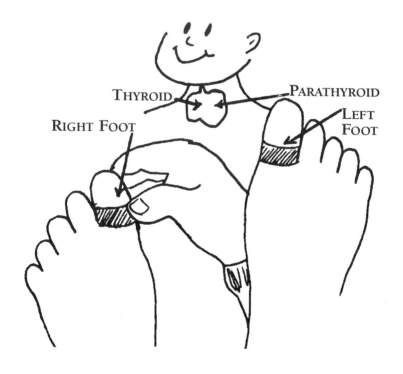

THYROID

PARATHYROID

RIGHT FOOT

LEFT FOOT

The **thyroid gland** controls how fast our body uses fuel. If we burn fuel too slowly, we gain weight. If we burn fuel too quickly, we lose weight.

This gland controls bone growth and helps keep our skin healthy.

The **parathyroid gland** is actually located inside the thyroid. It helps control the calcium and phosphorous in our blood which helps blood clot if we hurt ourselves.

It also works to keep our muscles relaxed, so we don't get muscle cramps.

The Adrenal Glands

These busy glands have about 50 different tasks to perform in our body. They help move blood around in the muscles. They also

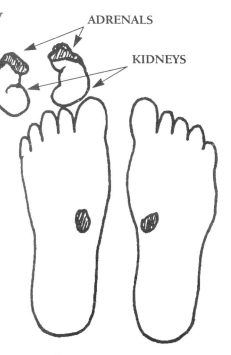

regulate our breathing, slowing down our breathing when we are relaxed and helping to speed up our breathing for when we are running or jumping.

They help in our digestion and in getting rid of waste products from our body.

The adrenal glands make a hormone, an important substance called **cortisone**.

Cortisone helps take soreness out of joint areas. It also protects our body's organs and tissues from too much stress.

Reflexology treatment on these glands is important if you have any allergies or asthma.

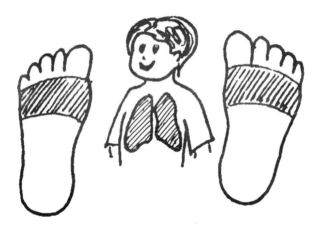

Our lungs are very important in keeping us alive. As we breathe in oxygen from the air, our lungs help distribute the oxygen into the blood and throughout our body.

As we breathe out, our lungs send out carbon dioxide, a waste product, from our body.

The Lymphatic System

The lymphatic system is made up of a system of tiny roadways, or vessels. They look just like a road map, sending roadways all over our body.

These vessels contain a clear fluid that bathes all of our cells and feeds them with nutrients taken from the small intestine.

Within the lymph system are little filtering stations called *nodes*. The nodes make antibodies to help our body fight disease.

The **lymph fluid** helps remove dead tissue, dead bacteria and other waste products from our body.

Our **spleen** makes antibodies and filters lymph fluid like the lymph node. The spleen stores extra blood, removes deformed red blood cells that cannot be used in the body and helps make **hemoglobin**, a substance that carries oxygen to the tissues.

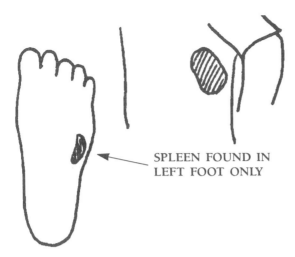

The **thymus gland**, located in the upper central part of our chest behind the breastbone, works hard to help us develop a strong immune system. In this way, we will stay healthier throughout our life.

THYMUS

The Digestive System

The digestive system has the job of making the food we eat available to every organ, nerve tissue and cell of our body.

The digestive system is made up of the stomach, the liver and gallbladder, the pancreas and the small and large intestines.

Our stomach receives the food we chew and swallow.

STOMACH

PANCREAS

The food is mixed with a special substance called **gastric acid.** This acid breaks up the food particles into a type of mush which is easy for the rest of the body to use.

The liver is our filtering system. Its job is to remove any drugs, alcohol, chemicals and the like from what we put in our body.

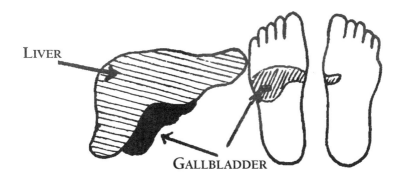

Bile is made in our gallbladder, and together with the liver, the bile helps break down proteins, carbohydrates and fats from our food, helping them move more easily through our bloodstream to various parts of our body.

Food particles then move into the small intestine. The small intestine keeps certain nutrients from the food to send out into the body, and other particles are sent into the blood and lymph systems to be removed from the body.

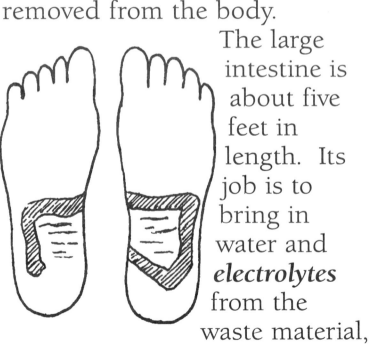

The large intestine is about five feet in length. Its job is to bring in water and *electrolytes* from the waste material, which is stored inside of it until you have a bowel movement.

The Urinary System

Another system to eliminate waste material from our body is the urinary system. This system is made up of the kidneys, ureter tubes and bladder.

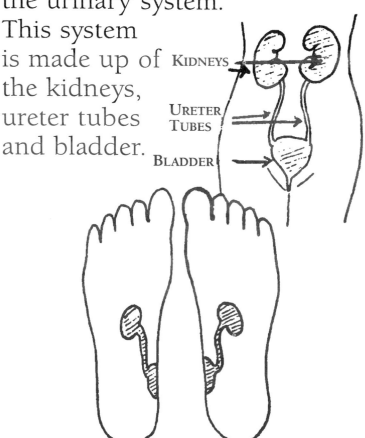

KIDNEYS

URETER TUBES

BLADDER

The urinary system is the main disposal unit of our body.

The most important organs of the urinary system are the kidneys. They help purify our blood and keep an eye on the amount of fluid passing through our body.

The kidneys strain fluid from our blood, separating waste products from nutrients to be used in our body.

They help produce more red blood cells when we need them, balance the acid and alkali in our body and watch over the amount of salt and other substances in our blood.

The ureter tubes are like hoses connecting the kidneys to the bladder, allowing urine to pass from the kidneys to the bladder.

The bladder is a reservoir, a kind of holding tank for the urine. When our urine reaches a certain level in the bladder, nerve fibers send messages to our brain that send us to the bathroom.

The Circulatory System

The circulatory system is responsible for blood and other body fluids to move through our body.

Our heart is the most amazing pump in the world. Each day it

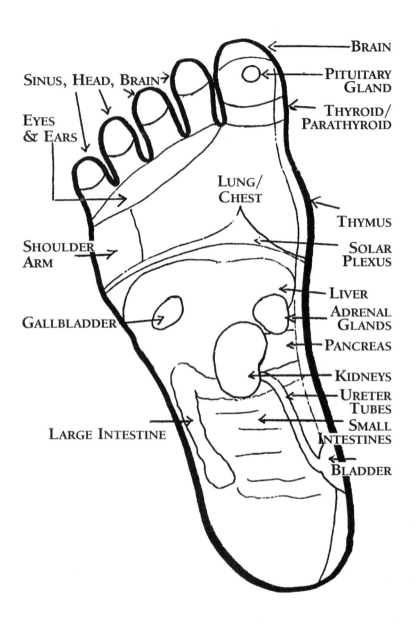

BRAIN

PITUITARY
GLAND

SINUS, HEAD, BRAIN

THYROID/
PARATHYROID

EYES
& EARS

LUNG/
CHEST

THYMUS

SHOULDER
ARM

SOLAR
PLEXUS

LIVER

ADRENAL
GLANDS

GALLBLADDER

PANCREAS

KIDNEYS

URETER
TUBES

LARGE INTESTINE

SMALL
INTESTINES

BLADDER

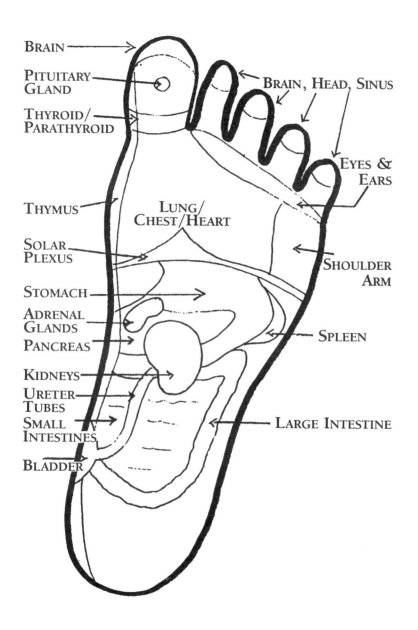

BRAIN

PITUITARY GLAND

THYROID/ PARATHYROID

BRAIN, HEAD, SINUS

EYES & EARS

THYMUS

LUNG/ CHEST/HEART

SOLAR PLEXUS

SHOULDER ARM

STOMACH

ADRENAL GLANDS

PANCREAS

SPLEEN

KIDNEYS

URETER TUBES

SMALL INTESTINES

LARGE INTESTINE

BLADDER

31

beats about 100,000 times.

The heart keeps our blood moving through our body, carrying nutrients, hormones, vitamins and **antibodies** (the Pac-Man of our body) to fight infection. It provides heat and oxygen to the tissues and takes away all the waste products from the tissues as it leaves.

The Pancreas

Hidden behind the stomach, the pancreas helps the stomach digest food. This gland makes **insulin,** which controls the blood sugar level in our body. **Glucose** is a type of energy food we need in our daily activities.

Our body can develop problems if the glucose level is not balanced.

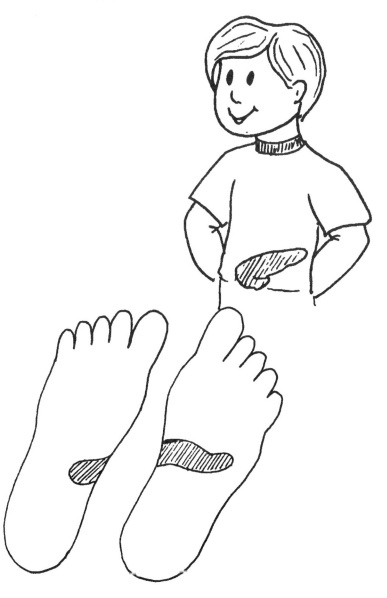

The Reproductive Organs

The reproductive organs of boys and girls are very different. However, the organs of both boys and girls produce a special kind of hormone that affects every cell in our body.

These organs help us develop into a boy or girl and help us become parents as we mature.

Reproductive organs are different for boys and girls but are found in same places on the feet

A Reflexology Treatment

There are many different viewpoints on where to start, and how to work on your feet so every important reflex is covered. As you work on your feet, you may want to work longer in certain areas that are sore.

Begin by working on the top of your toes.

Work down the sides and back and front of each toe, paying particular attention to your big toe. Work all the way from the tops of your toes to the place where your toes join the top of your foot.

Press in the center of your big toe — to stimulate your **pituitary gland.**

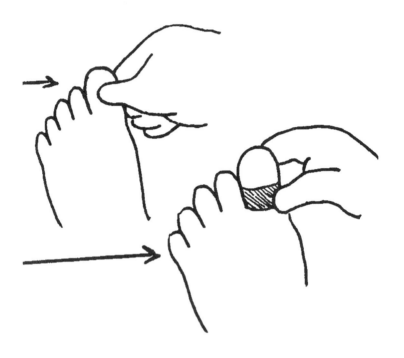

Press along the back of your big toe where the toes join your foot. This is the area of your **thyroid** and **parathyroid glands** —very important glands, second only to the pituitary.

Work along the very top of your foot, at the place where your foot and toes meet. This is for your **eyes** and **ears.**

Now work down from where your toes connect with your feet, down to just under the ball of your foot (see picture below). Work in lines, moving from top to bottom, until you have pressed in on the entire area. This is all of your upper

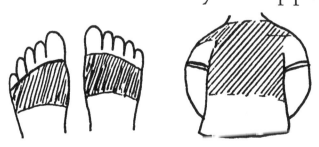

chest area — **lungs**, **heart**, **thymus**, **shoulders** and **upper back**.

Work across the area just before you move into the area of your arch. This is your **solar plexus** — the area where you sometimes feel butterflies in your stomach just before a big test at school.

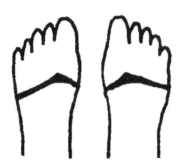

The *lumbar* nerves are located in your lower back area and help your legs and feet.

The *sacral* nerves take care of your pelvic and buttock areas.

As you can see in the picture, when you want to work on your spine, for a **backache**, **headache** or such, you would walk your thumb along the inside, big toe edge of each foot from the top of your big toe to the middle of your heel.

There are six very important glands in our body which send messages through the bloodstream all over our body.

When a gland is out of balance, it can affect our entire

body, interfering with our growth, our body weight, our energy levels and our mental and physical health.

When a gland is out of balance, our body is out of balance.

The Pituitary Gland

The pituitary gland is in charge of all the other glands in our body. It is located in our brain.

The reflex point on our feet is in the center of our big toes. Give this point a little push.

This gland is in charge of our growth, telling our cells to work faster or slower. It over-sees the arteries to make sure they are working properly, and controls the amount of water in

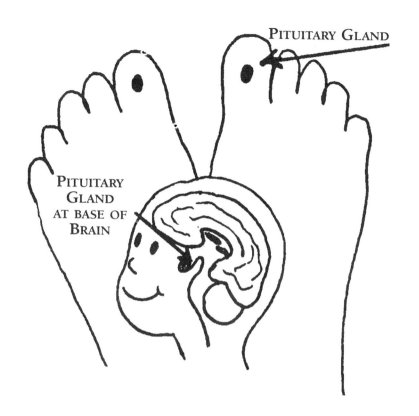

PITUITARY GLAND

PITUITARY
GLAND
AT BASE OF
BRAIN

our body to make sure it is
properly distributed to wherev-
er it needs to go.

The pituitary gland also regu-
lates, or controls, our blood
pressure and helps our body
get ready for the time when we
will become parents.

The Thyroid & Parathyroid

These glands are located in the front of our throat at the little hollow place where our neck connects to our shoulders.

Our Brain

Our brain is divided into two parts called **hemispheres**. The right portion controls the left side of our body. The left part of the brain controls the right side of our body.

When we work on the brain in reflexology, we work on the left toe for problems in the right side of the brain and on the right toe for problems on the left side.

So, if your head hurts on the right side, you would press on

your left toe to help your head
feel better.

Our brain is like a control
computer. It controls what we
see, hear, taste, touch and
smell. It controls the glands

and organs in our body — our heart, our lungs and other important parts that keep us alive.

Our brain controls the movement of our arms and legs — helping us run, walk, skip and jump.

Sometimes there are problems in the brain, and these parts of our body no longer move. It is called **paralysis**. In many cases reflexology can help people who are paralyzed regain full use or partial use of their body that did not function before treatment.

The Spinal Cord

Our spinal cord is an extension cord from our brain. It is protected within the bones of our spine. Nerves travel out of our spinal cord into every part of our body.

The *cervical* nerves in our neck control our neck and arms.

The *thoracic* nerves in our middle back control our chest and stomach areas.

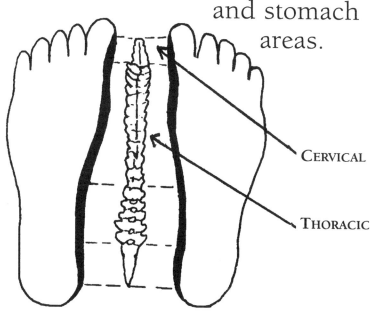

CERVICAL

THORACIC

When Your Body Needs Special Attention. . . .

Many times as we grow up we catch a cold, the flu, a sore throat, an earache and the like.

When we become ill, our body is telling us that it is out of balance. Some part of our body needs more energy.

Working on the reflex points on the bottom of your feet can help bring your body back into balance much faster, helping to prevent you from having to visit your family doctor or take medicine.

Working on your feet every day helps keep your body healthy and in balance, so you do not become ill.

When you do not feel well, you should work on your feet at least once, if not several times a day, sending as much healing energy as possible to the affected area.

Before you know it, you'll be feeling great!

As we grow up, we often have to deal with some very common ailments. These problems are easily helped or eliminated by working regularly on your feet. The pictures show you what part of your feet to work on in order to help you get better fast.

Allergies

- Work on the **adrenal glands**, **reproductive glands** and **pituitary gland** each day.

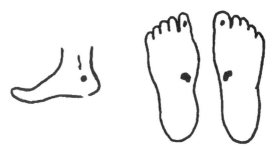

Asthma

- Work on the **adrenal glands**, your **large intestine**, **solar plexus** and **lungs**.

Backache or Pain From Fall

• Work the entire area of your **spine** along the inside edge of your feet from the big toe down to the tip of your heel. Work on this area several times a day.

• If your back hurts mostly in the upper part, work around the edge of the balls of your feet.

• If the middle of your back hurts the most, work the area opposite your arch on both your feet.

• If the pain is in the lower part of your back, work along your heel areas the most.

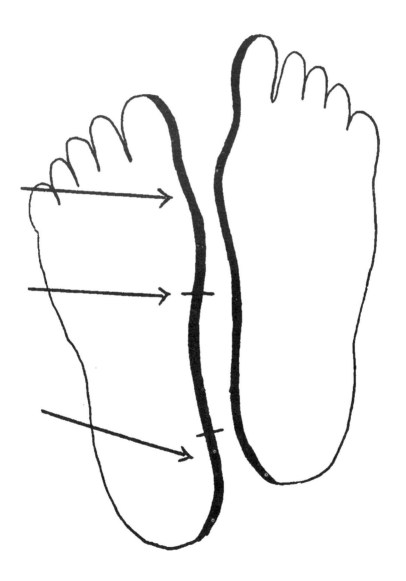

Neck

When you have pain in your neck, you can also have pain in your shoulders, or a headache.

• Work all your toes, the **shoulder** area on the part of your feet just under the little toe and the next toe.

• Also, work on the **solar plexus** area between the balls of your feet and the arch areas.

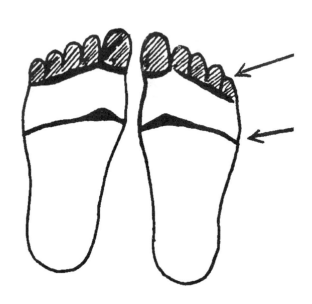

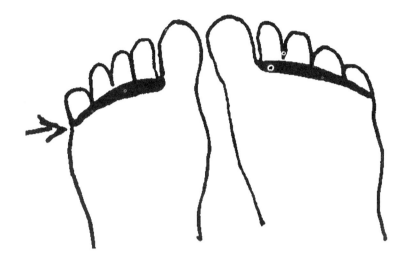

Earache

An earache is no fun at all. It can be quite painful and keep you awake all night long.
• To help an ear problem, work on the **ear** and **eye** reflex points just at the top of your foot where the toes join your feet.

Eyes

Do your eyes feel tired? Do you have poor vision and have to wear glasses or contact lenses?

Do your eyes bother you from pollutants in the air? From the wind? The sunlight?

To make your eyes feel better, work on your **eye** and **ear** points along the top of your

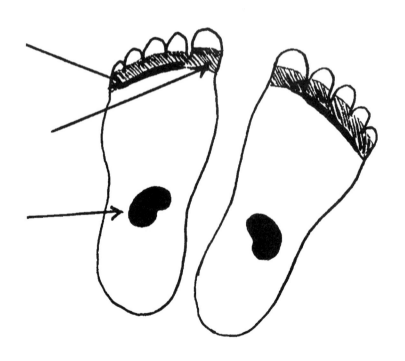

feet just where the toes and foot connect.

• Work all of your toes and the outside of your big toes from the top of your toes to where your big toes join your feet.

• Then work on the kidney reflex points. This will help eliminate any toxins in your body affecting your eyes.

Fever

When you have a fever, it is usually a sign that your body is fighting bacteria or a virus of some sort.

• To help bring your temperature back to normal, you should work on the pituitary gland points in the center of your big toes. Work every half hour until your fever begins to drop.

The pituitary gland is in charge of helping your body feel better when you have a fever. As soon as you begin to

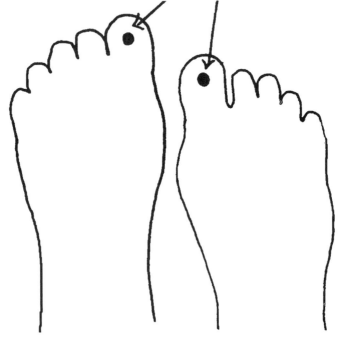

tell this important gland you need help, it will move into action and help you feel better quickly!

• Be sure to work the rest of your foot areas as soon as your fever drops, and you begin to feel better. You want to be sure all of your body's organs are balanced and all the dead bacteria and other waste products are eliminated from your body.

Headache

• Work on your toes from the tops down to where they join your feet.

• Work along the side of your big toes, from the top of the toes to where they connect with your feet.

• Work along the **solar plexus** area, just between the balls of your feet and your arches.

• Then work along your heels to give an extra amount of love to your **lower spine** areas.

Did you know many headaches are caused by problems in your lower back and tailbone areas?

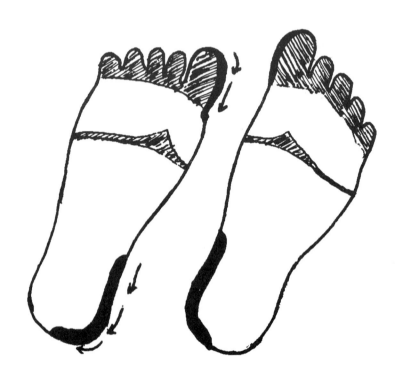

Sinus

• Work on your toes just as you would if you had a headache, and many times when your sinuses are bothering you, you do have a headache.

• Also work in the heel areas and the middle part of your feet for your **large intestine**. Work the **adrenal gland** areas and on your big toes, in the center, to call the **pituitary gland** into action.

Sore Throat

• Work your **neck** area in your toes, and in particular, the side of your big toes from the top to where it connects with your feet.

• Work the **adrenal glands** and the outside part of your feet from the little toe to the end of the heel. This will flush any infection out through your lymph system.

About the Author

The '80s were a decade of self-discovery for Leia Stinnett after she began researching many different avenues of spirituality. In her profession as a graphic designer she had become restless, knowing there was something important she had to do outside the materiality of corporate America.

In August 1986 Leia had her first contact with Archangel Michael when he appeared in a physical form of glowing blue light. A voice said, "I am Michael. Together we will save the children."

In 1988 she was inspired by Michael to teach spiritual classes in Sacramento, California, the Circle of Angels. Through these classes she had the opportunity to work with learning-disabled children, children of abuse and those from dysfunctional homes.

Later Michael told her, "Together we are going to write the Little Angel Books." To date Leia and Michael have created thirteen Little Angel Books that present various topics of spiritual truths and principles. The books proved popular among adults as well as children.

The Circle of Angels classes have been introduced to several countries around the world and across the U.S., and Leia and her husband Douglas now have a teacher's manual and training program for people who wish to offer spiritual classes to children. Leia and Michael have been interviewed on Canadian Satellite TV and have appeared on NBC-TV's Angels II – Beyond the Light, which featured their Circle of Angels class and discussed their books and Michael's visit.

The angels have given Leia and Douglas a vision of a new educational system without competition or grades — one that supports love and positive self-esteem, honoring all children as the independent lights they are. Thus they are now writing a curriculum for the new "schools of light" and developing additional books and programs for children.

Other Books by Leia Stinnett:

A Circle of Angels
The Twelve Universal Laws

The Little Angel Books Series:
The Angel Told Me to Tell You Good-bye
The Bridge Between Two Worlds
Color Me One
Crystals R for Kids
Exploring the Chakras
One Red Rose
When the Earth Was New
Where is God?
Who's Afraid of the Dark?

All My Angel Friends (Coloring Book)